EVERLASTING
Light

EVERLASTING
Light

A Resource for
Advent Worship

Sandy Dixon

Chalice Press.
St. Louis, Missouri

Cover art: Wreath photo by Skjold
Cover: Michael H. Domínguez
Art direction: Michael H. Domínguez
Interior design: Wynn Younker

This book is printed on acid-free, recycled paper.

Visit Chalice Press on the World Wide Web at
www.chalicepress.com

10 9 8 7 6 5 4 3 2   03 04 05 06 07 08

Library of Congress Cataloging–in–Publication Data

Dixon, Sandy
Everlasting light : a resource for Advent worship / Sandy Dixon.
82 p. ; 22 cm.
Includes bibliographical references.
ISBN 0-8272-0816-2 (alk. paper)
1. Advent 2. Worship programs
BV40 .D58 2000
263'.912 21
                                                        00009353

Printed in the United States of America

CONTENTS

Introduction   1

Hanging of the Greens   5

Year A   13

Year B   31

Year C   51

Christmas Sunday   69

Additional Resources   72

INTRODUCTION

Christians celebrate Advent within a paradox. Advent is the beginning of the Christian story, the preparation, the hope that the birth of our Savior brings. And yet, unlike a work of fiction, we know the end of the story. We celebrate the beginning of the story with the end in mind. We are preparing still for the coming of Christ, again and again. Jesus has already been born; he taught, lived, died, and rose from the dead. He comes again, and within each Advent we live in that expectation and hope, not only of the here and now, but of the second coming. We learn from the Advent scripture lessons how to live within that framework. The Advent readings "express not merely expectation of Christ's nativity, which has already happened, but the coming of Christ to rule, to judge, and to save. The hope in which the church participates and the expectation we share are of the kingdom come."[1]

John Westerhoff reminds us that "it is difficult to wait in hope. Yet Advent provides us with a moment to reflect on where Christ is trying to break into our lives and into our world. It is time to ask, Are we watching, are we expecting, are we ready to see it? Do we really want it to come?"[2]

Advent is the time to focus on the "word of hope, the possibility of birthing new life, a rekindled vision to which we might give our lives. Advent focuses on the paradoxes of longing anticipation and patient watching; transforming the way we envision life and yet living prepared; living out a wait for what never seems to come and continuing in hopeful trust; desiring to give up control and opening ourselves to new possibilities for life."[3]

In the Northern Hemisphere, Advent comes in the darkest time of the year; the Winter Solstice is in the middle of this season of the church year. Yet, for the church this is the season of light. We light a candle each Sunday to put out the darkness, to witness to the light to the nations. This light comes into the world and will never be put out. And each week the sanctuary is brighter. The darkness retreats as hope moves forward.

1

Using **Everlasting Light:**

Advent is the beginning of the church year. It is a time of reflection, preparation, and penitence as we wait for the birth of our Savior. Advent is celebrated in many congregations by the lighting of a candle in the Advent wreath each Sunday. The liturgical colors for Advent are purple or blue and can be used in paraments, stoles, and altar cloths. The candles in the Advent wreath can be all blue, all purple, or three purple and one pink. There are differing traditions of lighting the pink candle on the third or fourth Sunday to represent Christ as the perfect rose, or on the third Sunday for joy.

Everlasting Light: a Resource for Advent Worship contains services encompassing Advent worship.

- The Hanging of the Greens traditionally occurs in many churches on the first Sunday of Advent. The service in this book may be used during the Sunday morning worship. More detailed instructions are in that section.
- For each Sunday in all three cycles of the Revised Common Lectionary, including the Sunday after Christmas, the book provides materials for the lighting of the Advent candles.
- The service begins with a Litany of Light, a brief meditation, and a unison prayer. In addition, this book includes a prayer for communion, offering, ideas for a children's sermon, and a benediction. These resources use as their basis the scriptures from the Revised Common Lectionary. The user will find these scriptures used in the Litany of Light, prayers, and benedictions.
- For the congregations who want to do an Advent candlelighting during the children's sermon, the book includes three years' selections. These are not based on the lectionary. When the Advent candlelighting is done during the children's moment, use other parts of each Sunday's worship resources in *Everlasting Light,* leaving out the meditation.
- The source of scripture listings in this volume is The Revised Common Lectionary, developed by the Consultation on Common Texts and published in 1992.

"If the church is to be a gift to those whose lives cry out for good news, it will need to rethink how it integrates the stories of people with *its* story during the Advent season. This in turn will mean reflecting more deeply on the stories of Advent and more honestly on the stories of our lives."[4] John Westerhoff's words summarize the purpose of *Everlasting Light.* By the repeated hearing of the Advent lections in the Litany of Light, the sermon, the children's sermon, and the meditation for candlighting, worshipers will find a connecting point between the scriptures and their own lives. The candlelighting meditations in *Everlasting Light* give each hearer a responsibility in responding to God's initiative to bring God's reign to bear on the created order.

From Isaiah's words (60:19),

"but the LORD will be your everlasting light,
and your God will be your glory"

spoken in hope for the Hebrew people, to the fulfillment of which we sing each Christmas,

"O little town of Bethlehem, how still we see thee lie!
Above thy deep and dreamless sleep
the silent stars go by.
Yet in thy dark streets shineth the everlasting light;
the hopes and fears of all the years
are met in thee tonight"[5]

we know that in spite of the darkness of the winter season and the darkness present in the world, the light shines. The weeks of Advent with the emphasis on preparation, waiting, and watching help us know that God's light does shine in the darkness. The celebration of Christmas confirms the eternal light in God through Christ Jesus.

Let the light shine!

---

[1]Hoyt Hickman et al., The New Handbook of the Christian Year (Nashville: Abingdon Press, 1992), p. 52.

[2]John Westerhoff III, *A Pilgrim People: Learning Through the Church Year* (Minneapolis, Minn.: Seabury Press, 1984), p. 47.

[3]Westerhoff, p. 43.

[4]Westerhoff, p. 44.

[5]Words by Phillips Brooks (1868).

HANGING OF THE GREENS

Many congregations decorate the sanctuary for the Advent season in a service called Hanging of the Greens. The following service is intended to be used during morning worship on the first Sunday of Advent. Texts about the various customs, decorations, and symbols of the Advent season are included, woven in among the elements of worship. Although the hymnody of Advent does not normally include Christmas hymns, this Sunday is an exception. It is appropriate to use the carols of the Christmas season in connection with the specific decoration or symbol being put into place.

The service relies on the participation of the worshipers to bring the decorations forward, or to place them in the sanctuary. This Hanging of the Greens service is lengthy enough that a sermon may not be indicated, although a brief meditation could be used. Although this service uses a specific order of worship, adapt it for your own tradition and style of worship.

Include all the worship resources in *Everlasting Light* for the First Sunday in Advent in the places where they are suggested for this First Sunday.

Plan and organize the service so that it will flow smoothly. You will want to have the decorations in place or ready to be placed as the service indicates. Be sure the members of the congregation know they are to participate; choose ahead of time the volunteers to help coordinate the service. Adapt the service according to what symbols and decorations are particular to your congregation. You may want to use several narrators to vary the voices.

Hymn numbers are from *Chalice Hymnal*.

Order of Worship[1]

Prelude

Call to Worship *(Use the Litany of Light from the First Sunday of Advent.)*

Invocation

Narration: The Decoration of the Sanctuary

During the Advent season, we prepare for the one who has come, whom we expect to come, and who will come again. In the Advent season, we recall God's entering history as one of us in his Son, Jesus Christ. We prepare our hearts so that God will find room and expression in our lives. As we proceed through Advent season, we pray for the day when every knee shall bow and every tongue confess that Jesus Christ is Lord. During Advent we look toward Christmas—the fulfillment of God's love for all people.

Through many generations we have had reminders of Jesus' birth in the beautiful symbols of music, customs, and tradition so that we will not forget what our God has done. In the Hanging of the Greens, we share with Christians through the ages the memory and anticipation of Christ's coming. We festively decorate our church with the symbols of life, joy, and hope.

Jewish children at the Passover celebration ask, "Why do we do this? What does this mean?" The story of the angel of death passing over the homes of the Hebrews is retold so that the generations will not forget that mighty act of God. Christian children will ask, "Why do we do this? What does this mean?" We tell the story again and then proclaim, "God is with us. Jesus Christ is born."

Opening Hymn: "O Come, O Come, Emmanuel" *(CH* 119)

Narration: The Paraments

(During this narration, put the pulpit antependia, bookmark, and communion table runner in place.)

For many months, during the Pentecost season or Ordinary Time, the color used by the church in the paraments has been green. Green symbolizes growth—in the Christian life for each individual and each place where the church has witness. During Advent, we change the paraments to purple—the color of royalty and of God's reign—in preparation for the coming of the Christ. (*Alt.:* During Advent, we change the paraments to blue—the color of hope. We wait for the coming of the Christ in eternal hope.)

On Christmas Eve, we will change the color to white, representing joy and the purity of Jesus Christ.

HYMN: "All Earth Is Waiting" (*CH* 139)

NARRATION: The Banners

(At this time, hang the Advent banners.)

Banners have long been a tradition in the Christian community. They provide a colorful representation of many Christian symbols. By linking visible symbolism to the seasonal themes or specific scriptures, they help us worship. We not only hear the themes of worship but can see them symbolized before us on the banners.

In Advent the rich colors of purple and blue are used in addition to the familiar symbols of Christ's coming. In preparation for worship, we are able to meditate upon the significance of this season as we are helped by these colorful additions to our sanctuary.

NARRATION: The Advent Wreath

(Place the Advent candles in the wreath at this time.)

The Advent wreath is a simple circle of evergreen branches. Because the branches come from outdoors during winter in the Northern Hemisphere, the evergreen testifies to the continuation of life. Bending the branches so that the ends touch to form a circle further symbolizes life without end.

Four candles encircle a central Christ candle. The candles signify God's Son as the light of the world. There are four candles for the four weeks in Advent. Each Sunday in Advent, we light the candles from the preceding weeks, along with a new one.

The Christ candle is not lit until Christmas Eve. The Advent wreath, with the increasing brightness from the candles, witnesses to the light that cannot be put out.

NARRATION: The Greens

(During the reading, congregational members will bring the garlands and boughs and decorate the sanctuary with them.)

Evergreens have long been considered symbols of eternity, a sign of God's everlasting nature, and an indication that the faithful will experience eternal life in communion with God in Jesus Christ.

The Advent custom of decorating with evergreen branches comes to us from the peasants of the Middle Ages, who believed that preparations should be made for the coming of Jesus. On the first Sunday of Advent, each family would gather evergreens and place them near the hearth in their home. We continue that tradition today as we hang the greens in our sanctuary, our church home.

As Isaiah 60:13 tells us: "The glory of Lebanon shall come to you, the cypress, the plane, and the pine, to beautify the place of my sanctuary." The evergreens we use to decorate our sanctuary will remind us of God's abiding love in Jesus Christ and of our eternal relationship with God.

NARRATION: The Wreaths

(The wreaths are to be hung at this time.)

Christmas greens had their origin in pagan cultures. Their use was incorporated into Christian worship by those who saw in them a deeper, richer meaning for the church. Laurel and bay symbolize victory and triumph. Yew and cypress point to eternal life. Mistletoe symbolizes peace. The prickly leaves of holly are the symbol of the crown of thorns. The circle shape of the wreaths uses the Christian symbolism of eternal God, eternal love, without beginning or end.

HYMN: "People, Look East" (*CH* 142)

NARRATION: The Word

The Word of God as we read from our Bibles is a love story between God and humankind. The Bible is a *storybook*. God has made a covenant with God's people. The covenant has been broken and then renewed over and over through history. God is Creator and Redeemer; God loves each one. In return, God expects us to love God, ourselves, and our neighbor. The Bible is also a *book of faith,* giving us direction in life. The Bible is a *book of revelation,* unveiling relationships with. God throughout time, that we might be witness to them. The Bible is a *book of vocation,* giving us a vision of how we are to live our lives in relationship with God and others.[2] This vision of how we are to live our lives comes to us as we listen to the Advent scriptures each week. It is clear we have a responsibility in fulfilling God's reign on earth.

THE READING OF THE WORD: Lessons for the First Sunday in Advent

GLORIA PATRI

THE CHILDREN'S SERMON *(Use this book's children's sermon starter from First Sunday for Year A, B, or C, as appropriate.)*

NARRATION: The Poinsettias

(Congregational members will bring the poinsettias to the chancel area at this time.)

The most popular flower of the Advent-Christmas season is the bright red poinsettia. This attractive flower was discovered growing wild in Mexico by Dr. Joel Roberts Poinsett, first American Ambassador there from 1825 to 1829. In Mexico, the plant was referred to as the "Flower of the Holy Night" or the "Flaming Leaf." Dr. Poinsett brought several of the plants to America, where they were developed into the type of flower we see today.

The poinsettia's symbolism is twofold. The star-shaped formation of red leaves reminds us of the star that shone on that first Christmas. The red flower reminds us of the blood of Jesus upon the cross, the Jesus who is our Savior.

Everlasting Light

PRAYER HYMN: "From Heaven Above" (*CH* 146)

PASTORAL PRAYER AND PRAYERS OF THE PEOPLE

NARRATION: The Christmas Tree

The Christmas tree is a wonderful sign of God's love and faithfulness. Never losing its green color, the Christmas tree reminds us of God's steadfast love, which endures forever.

Legend has it that Martin Luther was the first person to decorate his home with a Christmas tree. Luther was walking home one Christmas Eve when he saw the glitter of stars shining through the snow-covered branches of the fir trees. Luther was so awed by the sight that he took one of the trees home with him and placed candles on the branches, to demonstrate to his family what a glorious sight he had seen.

From this first Christmas tree in the Luther household, the custom spread. Now Christmas trees are used in homes, in churches, and in communities, wherever the birth of Christ is celebrated and the love of Christ is shared.

NARRATION: The Chrismons

The use of Chrismons on the tree began in the Lutheran Church of the Ascension in Danville, Virginia. Chrismons, or "Christ's Monograms," are handmade designs forming the familiar symbols of the Christian faith.

These symbols speak to Christians of the deep meaning of the gospel. The fish is the most ancient symbol for our Lord and was used as an easily recognized secret sign by early Christians. The first letters of the Greek words for *Jesus Christ, God's Son, Savior* form the Greek word for *fish.*

The Anchor Cross was called the cross of hope by first-century Christians; it reminds us that Jesus is the hope of the world. The *Chi Rho* combines the first two letters of *Christ* in Greek. The *x*-shaped *chi* reminds us of the manger of Jesus. The *rho* is shaped like a shepherd's crook and reminds us of the first visitors to the manger.

The star, angels, lambs, and other Christian symbols are used for Chrismons; each of them helps us recall the Christmas story.

(During the singing of the hymn, people place the Chrismons on the tree.)

HYMN: "It Came upon the Midnight Clear" (*CH* 153)

NARRATION: The Crèche

Perhaps the most well known of all the Christmas traditions is the scene of Bethlehem, where the birth took place. Many people were in the town, having registered for the census. There a stable was filled with animals and the sounds of the night. Shepherds, angels, wise men, and townspeople came to find the Christ Child.

Let us set the scene of the birth to keep before us during the Advent season.

(Congregational members may put the different parts of the manger scene in place during the singing of the hymn.)

HYMN: "O Little Town of Bethlehem" (*CH* 144)

NARRATION: THE ADVENT CANDLES

During Advent, we prepare by lighting candles each week. As we see the darkness of the world and the darkness of the winter season, we are witness to the Word of God come into the world—the light for all people. The light comes into the world, shines in the darkness, and is never extinguished by the world. Christ is the light of the world.

These candles are a visible reminder of the light and hope that Advent brings to us each year.

THE LIGHTING OF THE FIRST ADVENT CANDLE *(See below under First Sunday for Year A, B, or C, as appropriate.)*

UNISON PRAYER *(See below under First Sunday for Year A, B, or C, as appropriate.)*

HYMN: "One Candle Is Lit" (*CH* 128)

THE GREAT THANKSGIVING *(At this time the congregation shares the offerings and celebrates the Lord's supper.)*

CLOSING HYMN: "Come, O Long-expected Jesus" (*CH* 125)

BENEDICTION *(See below under First Sunday for Year A, B, or C, as appropriate.)*

---

[1]Adapted from a service by the Rev. Dr. Judith E. Ridlen, pastor of Northside Christian Church, St. Louis, Missouri.

[2]John Westerhoff III, *A Pilgrim People: Learning Throught the Church Year* (Minneapolis, Minn.: Seabury Press, 1984), pp. 4–5.

YEAR A

First Sunday of Advent

Isaiah 2:15. Psalm 122. Romans 13:11–14.
Matthew 24:36–44.

LITANY OF LIGHT *(from Isaiah 2)*

Come let us walk in the light of the LORD.
**Come, let us go up to the mountain of the LORD; that
he may teach us his ways and that we may walk in his
paths.**
During this Advent season show us how to walk in your
paths, O God of light.
**Peace be with all God's people; let us seek the well-
being of all creation.**

MEDITATION

Advent is a time to prepare, to get ready. It is a time for
watchfulness, reflection, and repentance. Advent is the beginning of a new life—the obvious example being that of
Jesus, the baby born at Christmas.

But maybe the less obvious new life is our own. Advent
is a time to begin our new life. Our scripture lessons for
today tell us that the time is *now!* Don't dilly dally; don't
wait for the rest of the crowd. Don't wait for the polls to be
in to select the more popular lifestyle. Change now. Our
instructions are clear. Put on the armor of light, live honor-
ably. Live peacefully, change weapons into instruments of
productivity. Put on the Lord Jesus Christ.

During this week, reflect, pray, then act. These instructions from today's lessons don't tell us to *think about what to
do;* they are clear-cut instructions about *doing.*

Go and do while we wait for the Christ.

Lighting of the First Advent Candle

Unison Prayer

Into a world filled with choices, you come, O Lord. We thank you that we have the opportunity to change our actions into ones that will bring your kingdom on earth. Amen.

Children's Sermon Starter

Lead the children in discussing where they hear the words "It is time…" Maybe it is time to wash up for a meal; maybe the teacher says, "It is time for recess!" Transition into Advent as being a "time" to prepare for Christmas. Ask them to watch for how the church prepares—for example, the Advent wreath, the decorating of the church facility, the Christmas program. Perhaps using the phrase "It is time to wait for Jesus to come" will help them understand this season. Close with prayer that all will rejoice with the coming of Jesus our Savior.

Offering Prayer

O Giver of life, accept these gifts we bring to you today. We have given in response to the great gift of your Son and our Savior. Use these gifts, we pray, that all may know your ways of love and peace. Amen.

Communion Prayer

O God of goodness, peace, and light, we come to your table today seeking the peace you want for your people. Help us make our swords into plowshares that we may nurture the earth and plant. Show us how to turn our spears into pruning hooks that we may reap bountifully. With the abundance of your feast set before us, the bread harvested from the wheat, the grapes from the vines, we remember your gift to us in your Son, Jesus Christ. In this season of preparation, let us walk by your spirit in goodness and light. Amen.

BENEDICTION AND BLESSING

Arise from darkness into this season of light. Because of our belief that salvation is near, it is day, it is light, it is Advent. Let us put on the armor of light. Amen.

Second Sunday of Advent

Isaiah 11:1–10. Psalm 72:1–7, 18–19.
Romans 15:4–13. Matthew 3:1–12.

LITANY OF LIGHT *(from Psalm 72 and Romans 15)*

Blessed be the LORD, the God of Israel, who alone does
wondrous things.
**May the God of steadfastness and encouragement
grant us to live in harmony with one another.**
Together, lift our voices to glorify the God and Father of
our Lord Jesus Christ.
**Blessed be his glorious name forever; may God's
glory fill the whole earth. Amen and Amen.**

LIGHTING OF PREVIOUS SUNDAY'S CANDLE

MEDITATION

Have you ever been the recipient of a surprise birthday
party? Or maybe you helped plan one for someone else.
What fun! The celebration was so unexpected. And that
unexpected surprise was what made it so memorable.

In our Hebrew Scripture lesson this morning, Isaiah tells
about many surprising things. First, a branch will grow out
of the seemingly dead stump of a tree. Then a meek lamb
will live with the fierce lion; a flesh-eating leopard will sleep
near a young goat. The author pairs several fierce animals
with meeker ones, including human children. On God's holy
mountain, all will be good. And who would expect a strange,
raving man clad in skins and eating locusts and wild honey
to tell us about Jesus Christ?…or for the Savior of all people
to come as a baby?…and from a horrible death on the cross,
a resurrection? In God's good world, all can be possible.

God is full of surprises! This week, the second in Advent, look around you for God's surprises. Let your heart be
open to be surprised by the God of us all as we get ready for
the Savior's coming.

16

LIGHTING OF THE SECOND ADVENT CANDLE

UNISON PRAYER

Prepare us for the coming of our Savior by opening our hearts to your wonderful works. Let us praise you as we discover all that you have done for us. Amen.

CHILDREN'S SERMON STARTER

Start by asking the children if they think a fierce lion can sleep next to a lamb. Would they be surprised if it could work? Guide their conversation from what would happen in our ordinary world to what will happen in God's reign. Any good thing is possible; God is full of wonderful surprises for God's people. Christ's coming is the biggest and most important surprise! Ask the children to share what surprises they might like to have in God's good world—and help them to see surprises not just for themselves but for others. Close with prayer that the children will be aware of God's goodness and that God will help them look for surprises as they wait for Christ's coming.

OFFERING PRAYER

O generous God, we are surprised in so many ways by your gifts. Your gift to us of your Son Jesus surpasses anything anyone could give to us. You held nothing back, but gave to us life itself. In preparation for the coming of your Son, we have offered these gifts to you and the service of your church. Amen.

COMMUNION PRAYER

"Lo, how a rose e'er blooming from tender stem hath sprung,
of Jesse's lineage coming by faithful prophets sung;
it came a flow'ret bright, amid the cold of winter
when half spent was the night.
Isaiah 'twas foretold it, the rose I have in mind;
with Mary we behold it, the virgin mother kind.
To show God's love aright she bore to us a
Savior when halfspent was the night."[1]

Blessed are you, God, for the wondrous things you have done for your people. You have sent to us a Savior in your Son, Jesus Christ. We celebrate the greatness of your love in coming to this table today. The bread and cup, the body and blood of your Son, are given to us by your grace. In the presence of the Holy Spirit, let us eat and drink these emblems set before us. Amen.

BENEDICTION AND BLESSING *(Romans 15:13)*

May the God of hope fill you with all joy and peace in believing so that you may abound in hope in the power of the Holy Spirit.

---

[1]"Lo, How a Rose E'er Blooming," German carol (fifteenth century), trans. Theodore Baker (1894).

Third Sunday of Advent

Isaiah 35:1–10. Psalm 146:5–10 or Luke 1:47–55.
James 5:7–10. Matthew 11:2–11.

LITANY OF LIGHT *(from Luke 1)*

God's mercy is for those who fear him from generation to generation.
He has shown strength with his arm; he has scattered the proud in the thoughts of their hearts.
He has brought down the powerful from their thrones and lifted up the lowly.
He has filled the hungry with good things.
God has helped his servant Israel, in remembrance of his mercy, according to the promise he made to our ancestors, to Abraham and to his descendants forever.
God, we thank you for keeping your promises of good news. We await your coming.

LIGHTING OF PREVIOUS SUNDAYS' CANDLES

MEDITATION

When you hear good news, what is the first thing you want to do? Isn't it instinctive to want to share it with others? There is a wonderful camp song in which the writer wants to shout the good news from the mountaintop!

Isaiah's whole scripture passage foretells good news for God's people. Wonderful things will happen. That is also evident in the gospel readings. Mary has just heard the good news that she will bear God's son, and she praises God!

Jesus is instructing people to tell John, who is in prison, the good news—that blind people can see; the lame are walking; the deaf are hearing; the lepers are cleansed; the dead are raised; and the poor have good news preached to them. All this good news has happened because Jesus has come!

The word *evangelism* means sharing the good news. When we share the good news of God's love as shown to us in Jesus Christ, we are evangelists.

During the coming week in Advent, as we get ready for Christmas, let's shout our good news from the mountaintop, or from our desk, the factory floor, the checkout counter, or the playground. Share with your friends, family, coworkers, teachers, and playmates the good news that Christ is coming.

LIGHTING OF THE THIRD ADVENT CANDLE

UNISON PRAYER

In this Advent season, we wait for your coming. Help us to recognize the good news that your coming brings. Give us courage and strength to share it with all your people. Amen.

CHILDREN'S SERMON STARTER

Begin the conversation by asking children if they can remember past good news. Maybe it was the arrival of a new brother or sister, or that they received a good grade in science. Ask how they told or shared that good news. Then lead them into the importance of sharing with others the good news that God loves us enough to send his Son, Jesus, to us. Remind the children that Advent is a time of waiting and preparing for Jesus' coming, the perfect time to share good news! Close with a prayer that the children will know they are loved by God and that they can share this love with others.

OFFERING PRAYER

O generous God, there is so much good news to share. We have been given a Savior and life eternal in your great love. Now we have given some of our gifts for the work of your church on earth. Bless these gifts that they will be used to spread that good news. Amen.

COMMUNION PRAYER

We are a fortunate people indeed, God. You have shared with us that which is most important to you—your Son. By his life, death, and resurrection we are given the good news of life eternal in your love. The loaf and cup before us tell of this love each time we come to the table. By the eating and drinking of the bread and wine, we commit ourselves to sharing what you have so freely given to us. Help us, Holy Spirit, to act in the name of our Savior, who comes again to us. Amen.

BENEDICTION AND BLESSING *(from James 5)*

Let us be patient until the coming of the Lord. Strengthen our hearts, for the coming of the Lord is near. We go into the world, knowing you are coming soon, God. Bless us as we go forth to tell your good news. Amen.

Fourth Sunday of Advent

Isaiah 7:10–16. Psalm 80:1–7, 17–19.
Romans 1:1–7. Matthew 1:18–25.

LITANY OF LIGHT *(from Psalm 80)*

We wait for your coming, God, into a world filled with strife.
Restore us, O God of hosts; let your face shine, that we may be saved.
We wait for your coming, God, into a world filled with hunger and homelessness.
Restore us, O God of hosts; let your face shine, that we may be saved.
We wait for your coming, God, into a world filled with unbelief and hopelessness.
Restore us, O God of hosts; let your face shine, that we may be saved.
Emmanuel, God with us, is our hope.
Let us follow the light that saves us.

LIGHTING OF PREVIOUS SUNDAYS' CANDLES

MEDITATION

A name is everything, they say. The name of a product has to make everyone want to try it. The name of a book should entice everyone to read it. If a manufacturer of a washing machine or freezer has a good reputation, that name says quality and trustworthiness. As we name our children, we want names that are popular and carry the aura of friendliness, authority, and leadership.

And what is God's child to be named? He could be a Moses after the one who led God's people to freedom; he could be a David after his great-plus grandfather who was a king. He could be an Isaiah after a prophet of hope.

But God's child was to be named Emmanuel. *Emmanuel.* God with us. What comfort in times of need and stress— God with us. What strength in times of challenges to our lives—God with us. What assurance at our baptism and

22

commitment—God with us. What peace at illness and death—God with us! God with us, always, forever, continually. God with us, filling us, guiding us, comforting us, encouraging us, giving us new possibilities.

Yes, Emmanuel. A great name for God's son! This week we go from the preparation for Christ's coming to celebrating the actual event. Let us remember what Emmanuel means as we celebrate later this week. God is with us!

LIGHTING OF THE FOURTH ADVENT CANDLE

UNISON PRAYER

Let us prepare our hearts, O God, for the coming of your Son, Emmanuel, into the world. Strengthen our faith, give us hope, and help us act in the name of the one who comes. Amen.

CHILDREN'S SERMON STARTER

See if the children have ever helped name a pet or heard their parents talking about the name for a younger sibling. Ask if they have ever heard the story of why they are named as they are. Maybe they have been named for a relative or a friend. Hear their stories about names. Talk about the names for God's Son. Remind them we call him Jesus, Lord, Christ. Tell them of a name they may not know: *Emmanuel.* Share what it means to have *God with us.* Close with a prayer that the children may always feel God's presence.

OFFERING PRAYER

Because we feel your presence with us always, because we are the receivers of life in you, because you sent your Son to be our Savior, we respond by the giving of ourselves to you in these offerings. Accept them, use them for your glory. Amen.

COMMUNION PRAYER

O God who is ever near us, in these final days before your coming, we offer our prayers to you. We thank you for life itself; we thank you for our church family. Most of all, we give you thanks for your Son, our Savior, Jesus Christ. In this meal today, we eat and drink in anticipation of the coming of the Christ. Help us to feel your presence, Emmanuel, God with us as we take the bread and cup. Amen.

BENEDICTION AND BLESSING *(from Romans 1)*

Go, prepare, wait for the coming of Jesus Christ. Remember what you have been told. God is with us.

Grace to you and peace from God our Father and the Lord Jesus Christ. Amen.

Christmas Eve

*(Any of the following scriptures may be used
on Christmas Eve or Christmas Day.)*

Isaiah 9:2–7	*Isaiah 62:6–12*	*Isaiah 52:7–10*
Psalm 96	*Psalm 97*	*Psalm 98*
Titus 2:11–14	*Titus 3:4–7*	*Hebrews 1:1–4, 5–12*
Luke 2:1–14, 15–20	*Luke 2:1–7, 8–20*	*John 1:1–14*

LITANY OF LIGHT

"Good Christian friends, rejoice
with heart and soul and voice!
Listen now to what we say: News! News!
Jesus Christ is born today."[1]
"O Sing to the LORD a new song;
sing to the LORD, all the earth.
Sing to the LORD, bless his name;
tell of his salvation from day to day."[2]
ALL *(with great feeling)*:
"Good Christian friends, rejoice
with heart and soul and voice!
Now you need not fear the grave: Peace! Peace!
Jesus Christ was born to save!
Christ was born to save! Christ was born to save!"[3]

LIGHTING OF PREVIOUS SUNDAYS' CANDLES

MEDITATION

Do you remember being a teenager and saying to a
parent, "You just don't understand!"? Do you remember a
saying from the late '90s attributed to God: "What part of
'*thou shalt not*' don't you understand?"

God's chosen people, the very ones God had called, just
didn't seem to understand what God meant by the laws or
instructions that God had given them. God spoke through
the prophets; God was present in the mighty acts of history.
But the people still didn't understand. Being God-apart-from-
the-people wasn't seeming to give God's people enough.

Do you remember being a parent of a teenager and saying to your child, "I was a teenager once too"? You are saying to them that you know what is like to be that age; you understand.

God sent Jesus, the beloved and only Son, so we could understand the laws, instructions, and directions better. God sent Jesus to be Emmanuel: God with us. Jesus showed us, taught us, lived among us. Jesus, God's Son, gave everything he had for us. By this gift, which surpasses any gift, God is saying to us, "I understand what it is like to live on earth. I was there with you."

Tonight we celebrate and affirm this gift to us. Emmanuel, God with us. God understands and loves us because God is among us.

LIGHTING OF THE CHRIST CANDLE

UNISON PRAYER

Tonight we worship in awe and wonder on this Christmas Eve. We give thanks that you cared enough for your people to come and live among us so that we might know your ways. Amen.

CHILDREN'S SERMON STARTER

(See the selections for Christmas Eve from the section at the end of this book entitled "Lighting the Advent Candles during the Children's Sermon Time.")

COMMUNION PRAYER

We thank you, loving God, for Jesus who came long ago as your beloved Child and who has come again in this feast of joy to be our light, our hope, our life. As we receive strength and spiritual nourishment from the bread and cup, let us be bearers of the everlasting light, messengers of eternal hope and witnesses to new life in you. Amen.[4]

OFFERING PRAYER

Giver of gifts, generous God, accept now our gifts to you for the furthering of your reign on earth. Bless us as givers; bless and multiply these gifts so that your will is done. Amen.

BENEDICTION AND BLESSING

"Love came down at Christmas,
Love all lovely, love divine;
Love was born at Christmas,
Stars and angels gave the sign."[5]
"He it is who gave himself for us
that he might redeem us from all iniquity
and purify for himself a people of his own
who are zealous for good deeds. Amen."[6]

---

[1]"Good Christian Friends, Rejoice," Latin (fourteenth century), trans. John Mason Neale (1853).

[2]Psalm 96:1–2.

[3]"Good Christian Friends, Rejoice."

[4]Adapted from *Thankful Praise* (St. Louis: Chalice Press, 1987), p.74.

[5]"Love Came Down at Christmas" by Christina Rossetti (1885).

[6]Titus 2:14.

Sunday after Christmas Day

Isaiah 63:7–9. Psalm 148. Hebrews 2:10–18.
Matthew 2:13–23.

LITANY OF LIGHT *(from Psalm 148 and Isaiah 63)*
Let us tell the gracious deeds of the LORD.
Let us tell all that the LORD has done for us.
We are God's people. God is our Savior.
We are saved by God's presence; we are redeemed.
Praise the name of the LORD, for his name alone is
exalted; his glory is above earth and heaven.

LIGHTING OF ALL THE CANDLES

MEDITATION

As you celebrated Christmas a few days ago, it is likely
that you remembered or shared a story of other Christmases.
Maybe you laughed as you remembered how Grandma
knocked over the Christmas tree as she watered it and that
you teased her about "snooping." Perhaps there were memories of your family's singing Christmas carols in the car while
driving around town looking at Christmas decorations. Then
there was the time your nephew played the baby Jesus in
the Christmas program and slept the whole time! And sadly,
we may remember the first Christmas without our parents
present.

For six weeks now, we have heard the prelude, the main
movement, and now the postlude to the Christmas story.
Think for a moment just how many years you have heard
the Christmas story. Just as one retells family stories, we
Christians retell our family stories. Our favorite seems to be
the Christmas story.

Each year we hear it, we hear it anew, and we are re-
minded once again that God loves us and sent his Son, Jesus—
the baby born at Christmas as God's gift to us—a great gift of
love. That's the good news we need to tell.

Let's keep telling the story!

UNISON PRAYER

O God who is the greatest giver of all times, we thank you for memories and families. We thank you for gifts and givers, for stories and storytellers. But most of all, we thank you for your love as given to us in our Savior, Jesus Christ. Amen.

CHILDREN'S SERMON STARTER

Ask the children to start at the beginning (that is, the angel and Mary for this exercise) and retell the Christmas story. Prompt when necessary. When they are through, tell them that this is an important story they can remember and share with others. Close with a prayer that they will remember the story and God's love for them in all that they do.

OFFERING PRAYER

"What can I give him, poor as I am? If I were a shepherd, I would bring a lamb; If I were a wise man, I would do my part; yet what I can I give him: give my heart."[1] God, we give to you our hearts, our lives, our gifts, and our talents. Thank you for your greatest gift; bless now these gifts we bring. Amen.

COMMUNION PRAYER

O Creator of love and life, we come to this table today full of the joy of Christmas. We are confident that your love and presence will not be put away like the bright decorations. We are confident that your gift to us, your Son and our Savior, will not be seasonal, going away when the holiday is over. This bread and cup are always here before us, as is your great love. We know this presence through your Son, Emmanuel, God with us. We feel your presence in the Holy Spirit as we eat and drink together in your name. Amen.

CARRYING FORTH THE LIGHT

(This Sunday the acolyte should relight the taper just before extinguishing the Christ candle, which is the last to be extinguished. When the acolyte goes back down the center aisle, those who are able should rise as the light passes.)

BENEDICTION AND BLESSING

Go, Christians. Tell the story of God's love and Jesus' birth. Let your words of good news be a blessing to others. May you be blessed in the words' telling with the presence of the God who is our Savior. Amen.

---

[1]"In the Bleak Midwinter" by Christina G. Rossetti (1872).

YEAR B

First Sunday of Advent

Isaiah 64:1–9. Psalm 80:1–7, 17–19.
1 Corinthians 1:3–9. Mark 13:24–37.

LITANY OF LIGHT   *(from Isaiah 64 and Psalm 80)*

Come, wait for the LORD's coming as we begin the Advent Season.

How do we know it is the time for the LORD to come? What signs will we see?

Hear the word of God spoken to help us know the coming Christ.

From ages past no one has heard, no ear has perceived, no eye has seen any God besides you, who works for those who wait for him. Restore us, O LORD God of hosts; let your face shine, that we may be saved. We are your people!

MEDITATION

Do you remember a time, maybe when you were a child, when you were so excited that you could hardly wait for something to happen? It was hard to sleep at night because you were so excited. Did you ever wait for someone special to come to see you, and you stood or sat at a window to watch for them to pull into the driveway? You weren't exactly sure what time they would come, but you wanted to be ready!

Advent is about waiting and being ready. We are waiting for the Christ to come. Again. We have had many Advents and Christmases. Yet the waiting is no less significant. The waiting gives us time to get ready. We must be always alert, awake, and excited. We must watch in our daily lives this Advent, as during the whole year, for ways the Christ enters our lives. As we wait for God, we can know that God works in our lives. And we know that we are God's people and can wait in hope.

Unison Prayer

God and Father of Christ our Savior, help us as we wait for the coming again of the baby Jesus. Keep us alert, awake, and aware of the times in our lives when we know your salvation. Even more, help us to share that good news of salvation with others. Amen.

Children's Sermon Starter

Ask the children if there is a day coming soon that they are excited about. The answer, even this early, will be Christmas! Talk with them about waiting and being excited. Christ's coming is worth being excited about. Guide them into thinking of ways they can wait and let others see that they are God's children by their actions. Close with prayer thanking God for choosing the children as God's own, asking that God guide their actions and words during this season of waiting.

Offering Prayer

"In the places where we are broken, in the dark holes where something is missing, in the silence of unanswered questions, the wondrous gift is given."[1] We are your people, God, and we thank you for your presence and our salvation. Because you have chosen us, we offer these gifts to you in thanksgiving. Use them, we pray, to help others to know you, so that they will rejoice in your coming once more. Use these gifts to give hope to the hopeless, love to the unloved, and healing to those who are broken. Amen.

Communion Prayer

Into a world of noise and confusion, you will come to us quietly, Lord Jesus, as a child. Into a world of darkness, you will bring light. Into a world of greediness and desire, you will come as the perfect gift—the gift of love from our Creator. Into a world filled with hunger and thirst, you will come to give us bread and wine so we will never have to spiritually hunger or thirst. As we wait for the coming of the Christ, let us take the bread and cup, remembering that sacrifice made in love for us. Fed and refreshed, we thank you, our Savior, for life anew. Amen.[2]

BENEDICTION AND BLESSING *(from 1 Corinthians 1)*

Go into the world. Wait for the Christ who is and is to come. You do not lack any spiritual gift as you wait. God gives you strength. God is faithful. Yes, go in this knowledge, in the fellowship of his Son, Jesus Christ our Lord. Amen.

---

[1]From Harriett Richie, "He'd Come Here," *Christian Century* (December 13, 1995).
[2]Michael E. Dixon and Sandy Dixon, *Fed by God's Grace, Year B* (St. Louis: Chalice Press, 1999), p. 7.

Second Sunday of Advent

Isaiah 40:1–11. Psalm 85:1–2, 8–13.
2 Peter 3:8–15a. Mark 1:1–8.

LITANY OF LIGHT *(from Psalm 85)*

Let us speak the words of old, the words that gave comfort to God's people.
Surely salvation is at hand for those who fear him, that his glory may dwell in our land.
MEN: Steadfast love and faithfulness will meet; righteousness and peace will kiss each other.
WOMEN: Faithfulness will spring up from the ground, and righteousness will look down from the sky.
The LORD will give what is good, and our land will yield its increase. Righteousness will go before him, and will make a path for his steps.
Let us keep these words in our hearts as we wait for the Lord.

LIGHTING OF PREVIOUS SUNDAY'S CANDLE

MEDITATION

Imagine yourself to be a pioneer in the nineteenth century. You have packed up what belongings you could fit into the covered wagon and have set out from the flatlands of central Illinois with your spouse and children to move west to the wonders and riches of California. With your horses and other livestock, you have slowly crossed the Mississippi, the Missouri probably twice. You have gone across the plains of Kansas and the flats of eastern Colorado. You see the famed mountains alarmingly near. Even though the guide is experienced in finding mountain passes, you and your family have no idea how you can get across. If only somehow those valleys and mountains could be made smooth, just like the plains you just crossed.

The prophet cried out that in preparation for the Lord, this is what should happen. The valleys would be evened out, the rough places made smooth. In our frantic lives this Advent, we can look for ways to smooth our own rough places, to even out our valleys. And even more, to seek out ways to help others do the same.

LIGHTING OF THE SECOND ADVENT CANDLE

UNISON PRAYER

As we prepare for your coming this Advent season, help us seek ways to let go of our frantic-ness that comes with the Christmas season. Help us find ways to make our preparations truly reflect your coming, God of promise. We rest in the assurance that you are with us, feeding us with your spiritual nourishment. Amen.

CHILDREN'S SERMON STARTER

Ask the children if they have seen work on a highway with large equipment smoothing out ridges, or if maybe they have played with trucks in a sandbox or dirt and have smoothed over the hills they made. See if they can tell which would be easier to travel on—the rough, hilly way or the smooth road.

Talk with them about how life is rough; give examples of being bullied, of having lots of homework, or of how some of God's children don't have enough to eat or homes in which to live.

Help them begin to understand that because Jesus came, our lives are smoother. Jesus loves us and helps us; we can help smooth the way for others by our own lives and our gifts. Close with prayer that the children can have a smooth way this week in preparation for Christ's coming.

OFFERING PRAYER

God, you sent your Son into a world that is filled with rough places. Life is sometimes difficult. Yet, because you gave us your Son, we offer our gifts to you. Use them, we pray, so that your work in the world will make life smoother for your people. Amen.

Everlasting Light

Communion Prayer

"Comfort, comfort you my people;
tell of peace, thus says our God;
comfort those who sit in darkness
bowed beneath oppression's load.
Speak you to Jerusalem
of the peace that waits for them;
tell them that their sins I cover,
and their warfare now is over.

Make you straight what long was crooked;
make the rougher places plain;
let your hearts be true and humble,
as befits God's holy reign.
For the glory of our God
now o'er earth is shed abroad;
and all flesh shall see the token
that God's word is never broken."[1]

The body and blood of God's Son, Jesus Christ; the bread and cup on this table are the token of God's word—never broken. Let us eat and drink, comforted by the love of our God. Amen.[2]

Benediction and Blessing *(from 2 Peter 3)*

Wait for new heavens and a new earth, where righteousness is at home. While you are waiting, strive to be found by him at peace, without spot or blemish; regard the patience of the Lord as salvation.

---

[1]"Comfort, Comfort You My People" by Johannes G. Olearius (1671), trans. Catherine Winkworth (1863), alt.

[2]Dixon and Dixon, *Fed by God's Grace, Year B*, p. 9.

Third Sunday of Advent

Isaiah 61:1–4, 8–11. Psalm 126 or Luke 1:47–55.
1 Thessalonians 5:16–24. John 1:6–8, 19–28.

LITANY OF LIGHT *(from Psalm 126)*

When the LORD restored the fortunes of Zion, we were
like those who dream.
Then our mouth was filled with laughter, and our
tongue with shouts of joy;
then it was said among the nations, "The LORD has done
great things for them."
The LORD has done great things for us, and we
rejoiced.
Restore our fortunes, O LORD, like the watercourses in the
Negeb.
May those who sow in tears reap with shouts of joy.
Those who go out weeping, bearing the seed for
sowing, shall come home with shouts of joy, carrying
their sheaves.
The LORD has done great things for us!

LIGHTING OF PREVIOUS SUNDAYS' CANDLES

MEDITATION

In today's Hebrew Scripture reading, the prophet Isaiah
tells us he had been anointed to do a number of tasks of
social ministry—ministry among the people who have no
hope: the prisoners, the oppressed, those who are held cap-
tive, and those who are grieving. To them he will proclaim
"the year of the LORD's favor."

What if we could proclaim this next year "the year of
the LORD's favor" or the century of the Lord's favor? We are
early in the new millennium; there is still time for this decla-
ration to come to pass. And what if we could not only proclaim it, but actually act on it? What would it mean for our
lifestyle? How would we act differently? Where are the places
where our belief and faith are really put into actions? Paul
tells us, among other things, to seek to do good to one another and to all.

But even more important, what would it mean for those people whom Isaiah mentions? It sounds like an overwhelming task. But Christians joining together with other Christians of other races, denominations, and locations *can,* not just *could,* proclaim the year of the Lord's favor. Advent is the time to prepare for just how we can do that!

LIGHTING OF THE THIRD ADVENT CANDLE

UNISON PRAYER

"Holy Spirit, Pow'r divine, fill and nerve this will of mine. Boldly may I always live, bravely serve and gladly give."[1] God, you have done so many great things for us. Let your Holy Spirit give us power to live out the Christian life so that others may know you. Amen.

CHILDREN'S SERMON STARTER

Ask the children if they have a favorite toy or stuffed animal or maybe a favorite friend or relative. Have them tell how they act around this favorite relative or treat the favorite toy. See if the children will agree that they act or treat their favorites pretty well. Transition to how they treat other children at school, their neighbors, or people they meet. Tell the children that God wants us to treat all people as if they are the favorite, with kindness, politeness, and respect, and that God wants us to help others.

Advent is a good time to begin acting as God wants us to act. Have them say with you, "Do good to one another and to all." Close with prayer that the children will feel God within them as they wait for Jesus' coming.

OFFERING PRAYER

Dear God, you have done great things among us. You have provided us with food and shelter, warmth and protection. You have brought freedom and hope to discouraged lives. You have sent Jesus the Christ to redeem us. In loving response we come to you with these offerings, praying that through them we might help bring light and hope into the lives of others. Amen.

COMMUNION PRAYER

Into a world filled with discord and injustice, oppression and bondage, hopelessness and despair, you have come, Lord. In this season of Advent, we hear the good news of salvation and hope. Because of your coming, we can sing praises in your name. This bread and cup before us are the fulfillment of the promise to your people, the symbols of a risen Savior. Let us share these emblems together, receiving the power to embody the liberating spirit of your Son, Jesus Christ. Amen.[2]

BENEDICTION AND BLESSING *(1 Thessalonians 5:23)*

May the God of peace himself sanctify you entirely; and may your spirit and soul and body be kept sound and blameless at the coming of our Lord Jesus Christ.

---

[1]"Holy Spirit, Truth Divine" by Samuel Longfellow (1864).
[2]Dixon and Dixon, *Fed by God's Grace, Year B*, p. 11.

Fourth Sunday of Advent

2 Samuel 7:1–11, 16. Luke 1: 47–55 or Psalm 89:1–4, 19–26.
Romans 16:25–27. Luke 1: 26–38.

LITANY OF LIGHT *(from Psalm 89)*

I will sing of your steadfast love, O LORD, forever;
**With my mouth I will proclaim your faithfulness to
all generations.**
I declare that your steadfast love is established forever;
and your faithfulness is as firm as the heavens.
**Happy are the people who walk, O LORD, in the light
of your countenance.**

LIGHTING OF PREVIOUS SUNDAYS' CANDLES

MEDITATION

Who are the people chosen by God to do God's work?
It is easy to think of well-known people like Mother Teresa,
Dietrich Bonhoeffer, Billy Graham, and Millard Fuller, the
founder of Habitat for Humanity. It is easy to think of pas-
tors who lead congregations to do God's will.

How does God choose people? If you think of Bible
people, you will notice that God seems to choose ordinary,
everyday people. In this week's Old Testament lesson, we
hear about David and in the gospel lesson, Mary. David was
a shepherd, the youngest son—an unlikely candidate for king.
Mary was a teenager; her parents were ordinary small-town
people. But God chose them. From David's lineage comes
the Christ; from Mary comes the Christ—all with God's wonderful presence.

God chooses each of us to work toward the coming of
the Christ. In this last week of Advent, let us accept the
challenge, remembering what the angel told Mary, "The Lord
is with you." Nothing is impossible with God. And as Mary
did, we will praise God for choosing us and remember that
God has indeed done great things for us.

LIGHTING OF THE FOURTH ADVENT CANDLE

UNISON PRAYER

Let us today, Lord, exalt your holy name and exult in the ways you reach out to us this Advent season. Let us share the joy with all we meet.[1] Amen.

CHILDREN'S SERMON STARTER

Ask the children if they know who God chooses to do God's work in the world. Name David and Mary from today's lessons. Sometimes it is people whose names we know, such as Mother Teresa. But most of the time, it is people who are ordinary, everyday people like those we know in the church. Have them name the ministers, the choir director, those who teach church school. Have them name their parents and grandparents. Then have each say, "I am (name), and I have been chosen by God, and I know God is with me." Close with a prayer that each will know that God is with her or him as we prepare for the coming of the Christ.

OFFERING PRAYER

We offer ourselves to you, God of David, of Mary, and of Jesus. We offer our lives, our service, our witness, and our gifts. Use us and what we bring to you this day for your holy reign on earth. Amen.

COMMUNION PRAYER

It's Christmas time, Jesus, and all over the world people are magnifying your great name, singing Magnificats to you, and coming to your house to worship you more often. It's like you are a celebrity!

We have to admit, Jesus, that sometimes we want to make you a celebrity...maybe if we lift you up high enough, we'll forget that when you were here on earth in the flesh, you walked with men and women who had dirt under their fingernails and broken lives. Maybe if we make you a big enough celebrity, we can keep you as our healing, loving, miraculous Savior and won't hear you asking us to walk, work, and witness among those with dirt under their fingernails and broken lives. Maybe if we focus on your shining light, we won't see our own dirty fingernails and broken lives.

Ever-present Jesus, at this table and through these elements of bread and wine, reveal your whole self to us. Set our feet on a path that leads us not to a celebrity Jesus, but to a brilliant star—a star that shines over a manger and causes us to kneel in humble adoration and praise for the one whose starlight shines into every darkness with hope and peace.

With starlight in our eyes and dirt under our fingernails we pray. Amen.[2]

BENEDICTION AND BLESSING *(from Romans 16)*

Go, witness to the light. God is with you. God will give you strength for the tasks. To the only wise God, through Jesus Christ, be the glory forever. Amen.

---

[1]Jo Carr, *Upper Room Disciplines 1993* (Nashville: Upper Room, 1993), p. 362.
[2]By Ben Bohren, in Dixon and Dixon, *Fed by God's Grace, Year B*, p. 13.

Christmas Eve

*(Any of the following scriptures may be used
on Christmas Eve or Christmas Day.)*

Isaiah 9:2–7	*Isaiah 62:6–12*	*Isaiah 52:7–10*
Psalm 96	*Psalm 97*	*Psalm 98*
Titus 2:11–14	*Titus 3:4–7*	*Hebrews 1:1–4, 5–12*
Luke 2:1–4, 15–20	*Luke 2:1–7, 8–20*	*John 1:1–14*

LITANY OF LIGHT   *(Isaiah 52:7–10 and Psalm 98:1a)*

How beautiful upon the mountains are the feet of the
messenger who announces peace, who brings good news,
who announces salvation, who says to Zion, "Your God
reigns."
**Listen! Your sentinels lift up their voices, together
they sing for joy; for in plain sight they see the return
of the LORD to Zion.**
Break forth together into singing, you ruins of Jerusalem;
for the LORD has comforted his people, he has redeemed
Jerusalem.
**The LORD has bared his holy arm before the eyes of
all the nations; and all the ends of the earth shall see
the salvation of our God.**
**O sing to the LORD a new song, for he has done
marvelous things!**

LIGHTING OF PREVIOUS SUNDAYS' CANDLES

MEDITATION

Probably artists have portrayed the Christmas scene more
than any other Bible story. Without much trying, we can
envision the scene. Whether it is from a painting, a story, a
song, or even a television show, we have "seen," so to speak,
this birth many times.

The scene is set well enough that we see the people and
hear the sounds—the barn or cave, lit at night by lamps or
torches; the animals making chewing sounds while Mary
and Joseph are talking quietly. Perhaps Jesus is crying or

nursing. The shepherds come excitedly, followed by townspeople. The Christmas star is bright in the sky. It is just as we imagined.

Imagine yourself somewhere in this scene. Where are you? Who are you? How do you respond?

This is the crux of the whole Christmas story: God has given us a Christmas present—God's only Son. What is our response? Where do we fit into the picture?

The scriptures we have heard this Advent give us, God's people, a challenge. These words give us direction in our lives for helping to prepare for the reign of God to come on earth. It can happen in our lifetime!

Step out of the picture now and go from Bethlehem into the world, telling this good news of great joy to all people. Christ our Savior has come!

LIGHTING OF THE CHRIST CANDLE

UNISON PRAYER

God of miracles, help us to be messengers of peace, evangelists who bring good news and tell of your salvation to all people. Amen.

CHILDREN'S SERMON STARTER

(See the selections for Christmas Eve from the section at the end of this book entitled "Lighting the Advent Candles during the Children's Sermon Time.")

COMMUNION PRAYER

Loving God, we come to you in this decorated sanctuary, celebrating the birth of Jesus Christ, our Lord and Savior. We gather at this table and we wonder. It seems like such a long distance from Bethlehem's manger to the upper room, to Calvary, to the empty tomb. Yet it is here that your love comes full circle. The love that gave us Mary's baby is the same love that gave us the teacher in the upper room who blessed the bread and the cup. Birth and death, life and new life, are all one as you, in Christ, are one with us. Amen.[1]

OFFERING PRAYER

Alleluia! Alleluia! We bring our offerings tonight in a spirit of thanksgiving and rejoicing for your great gift, O generous God. Help us remember always to give in this spirit of joy. Use these gifts that all your people will know the good news of salvation in your Son, Jesus Christ. Amen.

BENEDICTION AND BLESSING

Go now, into the world, as did the shepherds, praising and glorifying God. Amen.

---

[1]Dixon and Dixon, *Fed by God's Grace, Year B*, p. 15.

Sunday after Christmas Day

Isaiah 61:10–62:3. Psalm 148.
Galatians 4:4–7. Luke 2:22–40.

LITANY OF LIGHT *(from Psalm 148)*

Praise the LORD! Praise the LORD from the heavens;
praise him in the heights!
Praise him, all his angels; praise him, all his host!
Praise him, sun and moon; praise him, all you
shining stars!
**Praise him, you highest heavens, and you waters
above the heavens!**
Let them praise the name of the LORD, for he commanded
and they were created.
**He established them forever and ever; he fixed their
bounds, which cannot be passed.**
Praise the LORD from the earth, you sea monsters
and all deeps,
**fire and hail, snow and frost, stormy wind fulfilling
his command!**
Mountains and all hills, fruit trees and all cedars!
**Wild animals and all cattle, creeping things
and flying birds!**
Kings of the earth and all peoples, princes and all rulers of
the earth!
Young men and women alike, old and young together!
Let them praise the name of the LORD, for his name alone
is exalted; his glory is above earth and heaven.
**He has raised up a horn for his people, praise for all
his faithful, for the people of Israel who are close to
him. Praise the LORD!**

LIGHTING OF ALL THE CANDLES

MEDITATION

Did you ever wonder about Mary and Joseph after all
the hoopla had ended? There they were, miles from home,
in a barn where their firstborn had come into the world.

46

Baffled by visits from shepherds, chosen by God to be earthly parents of the Savior, their bewilderment must have been great. *What are we to do now?* they must have thought.

Instead of fretting about it, they went about being good Jews. The law called for them to have the child circumcised and then go to the temple for the rite of purification, to present their heavenly Son to the Lord. And so they went. There they met Simeon and Anna, whose words must have puzzled them even more. They not only heard praises about their son but also strange and ominous predictions.

And yet, after all this was over, Mary and Joseph returned home to Nazareth and began to live as most other parents did. There were daily tasks to be done. There was a child to raise. There were the Jewish laws to keep. And so they lived as good Jewish people, keeping the faith of the generations before them. Perhaps they remembered that Isaiah had said that the Lord God would cause righteousness and praise to spring up before all the nations. Perhaps they knew, more than we realize, that their earthly son, Jesus, and God's heavenly son, Emmanuel, was to be the one to put that into place. But in the meantime, life in Nazareth went on.

Life after Christmas must go on. The waiting is over; the celebrating is over; the special foods are either eaten or frozen. Decorations are put in boxes to be stored for another year. And for the rest of the year...?

Let us remember Mary and Joseph. They went about keeping the faith that they had been taught. In the ordinary time that is coming, and until next Advent, let each of us keep the faith as children of God and heirs of God's reign.

UNISON PRAYER

God, you are a parent to us all. Help us, like Jesus, to grow, to become strong, and to become wise in your ways. Amen.

CHILDREN'S SERMON STARTER

Ask the children if they can remember the words to "Away in a Manger." Have them sing the first verse and be ready to help them with the second. *(If you need help with singing or instrumentation, have a volunteer ready.)* Let them know that there is a third verse that can be a prayer throughout the year. Have the children repeat the words after you, then sing it together two times. Let the congregation know the page number in the hymnal and close with the children leading the worshipers in this prayer-hymn.

In case your hymnal doesn't have the third verse, here it is:
"Be near me, Lord Jesus, I ask thee to stay
close by me forever and love me, I pray.
Bless all the dear children in thy tender care,
and fit us for heaven to live with thee there."[1]

OFFERING PRAYER

We praise you, God, for many things this day. We praise you for creation, we praise you for your continued presence with us. Especially we praise you for your Son, our Savior. Because of our gratitude, we bring these offerings to you. Bless them, multiply them, and use them for your glory. Amen.

COMMUNION PRAYER

At your table this day, we come in thanksgiving for the gift we have received this week. Along with the other gifts this Christmas, the gift that has come from you, God, surpasses anything else we could ever receive. Out of your great love for us you gave us your Son, our Savior Jesus Christ.

At this table we remember another gift you gave us— eternal life. We eat the bread and drink from the cup in humble gratitude for the magnitude of these gifts, remembering the sacrifice Jesus the Christ made so that we might have these gifts. Amen.[2]

CARRYING FORTH THE LIGHT

(This Sunday the acolyte should relight the taper just before extinguishing the Christ candle, which is the last to be extinguished. When the acolyte goes back down the center aisle, those who are able should rise as the light passes.)

BENEDICTION AND BLESSING

"Savior, again to thy dear name we raise
With one accord our parting hymn of praise;
We stand to bless thee ere our worship cease,
Then, lowly kneeling, wait thy word of peace."[3]
God, dismiss us with your blessing and peace.
We know you will always be with us
because your name is Emmanuel! Amen.

---

[1]Anonymous (19th century).
[2]Dixon and Dixon, *Fed by God's Grace, Year B*, p. 17.
[3]"Savior, Again to Thy Dear Name" by John Ellerton (1866), alt.

Year C

First Sunday of Advent

Jeremiah 33:14–16. Psalm 25:1–10.
1 Thessalonians 3:9–13. Luke 21:25–36.

Litany of Light *(from Psalm 25 and Jeremiah 33)*

The prophet said, "The days are surely coming, says the Lord, when I will fulfill the promise I made to the house of Israel and the house of Judah."
We want to live in a way to prepare us for the coming of Christ. How shall we do that?
Let the writer of the psalms teach us.
Let us know your ways; guide us to walk in your paths.
Help us to find the truth; teach us, O God of our salvation.

Meditation

In the spring of 1997, people all over the world were fascinated by the night sky. Even without a telescope or binoculars, the Hale-Bopp comet was brilliant in the northwest sky. It was the most spectacular comet that this generation of people had ever seen. The comet was so bright that even city dwellers, surrounded by lights, were able to see it. In the dark rural countryside it was awe-inspiring!

Generations had waited and waited for the Messiah. "When will he come?" they wondered. "How will we know him? Will there be a sign to let us know he is here?" Like a comet in the night sky, the Messiah brings light to people. To us. As we wait during Advent, we have a task. We should live our lives in expectation, in anticipation of a world which we have the opportunity to make light-filled.

The light of the first Advent candle can remind us through this week of the light—our way of life.

LIGHTING OF THE FIRST ADVENT CANDLE

UNISON PRAYER

Come to us, Lord Jesus. As Advent is here, full of expectations and full of hope, help us to see the ways your promise is being fulfilled. Guide our lives in your ways. Use our waiting for the Christ to know you better, O God of Israel. Amen.

CHILDREN'S SERMON STARTER

See if the children can remember a time when it was very dark, maybe at night out in the country without any streetlights, maybe at home without a nightlight, or maybe on a tour of a cave when the tour guide shut off all the lights and said, "This is total darkness." Then have them imagine what one light does in the darkness. Even one light makes a difference.

Help them with the idea that being a Christian is like being a light in the darkness. We shine and guide others to Jesus. Tell them that this is the first week of Advent, a time of preparing and getting ready for Jesus to come, and during our waiting, we need to be lights so others will know about the coming of Christ. Close with prayer that the children will feel God's light in them as they wait for God's coming.

OFFERING PRAYER

Accept these gifts, O God of righteousness. Use them in your world, O God of justice, to bring hope to the suffering, to bring light to those in darkness, and to bring love to all. We wait in anticipation of your reign. Amen.

COMMUNION PRAYER

Renew us, O God, as we come to your table. We are a take-charge people who are uncomfortable trusting in a future that only you can control. We are a here-and-now people who have difficulty in preparation and planning, even when the one we are preparing for is your Son and our Savior, Jesus the Christ. Even when we can get our heads and hearts around preparing for the coming of the baby in Bethlehem, we are awkward and uncomfortable in thinking about Christ returning in glory. Teach us here at your table, dear God, that we may learn to trust you completely with our lives and that we may turn our will over to be guided by yours. For it is here at this table that we learn how Jesus Christ, in complete trust and love, offered himself for us. Through this bread we eat and this cup we drink, let us offer ourselves to your loving and gracious will. May your Spirit work within our hearts as we partake. Amen.

BENEDICTION AND BLESSING *(from 1 Thessalonians 3)*

Go forth into the world in light. May the Lord make you abound in love for one another and for all. May God strengthen your hearts in holiness that you may be blameless before our God and Father at the coming of our Lord Jesus. Amen.

Second Sunday of Advent

Malachi 3:1–4. Luke 1:68–79. Philippians 1:3–11. Luke 3:1–6.

LITANY OF LIGHT   *(from Luke 3)*

Although we try to walk in paths of light, we need more ways to prepare for the coming of Christ.
Make the paths and roadways of our lives straight.
Smooth over the rough places.
As we work to do these in preparation,
we and all people shall see the salvation of God.

LIGHTING OF PREVIOUS SUNDAY'S CANDLE

MEDITATION

Do any of you remember Fuller brushes? Most of the time it was a man who would call on households periodically, selling Fuller brushes and household cleaners. People probably thought that Fuller was the name of the founder of the company. And it is. But the name *fuller* also implies clean. The fuller's job in Bible times was to prepare the wool after it was shorn from the sheep, to clean it. So the name of the company—Fuller—also implied cleanliness. What a lucky coincidence.

The last book of the Old Testament, Malachi, speaks of preparing. A messenger will make things ready. Using images from everyday life, the prophet speaks of a refiner's fire to purify the metals and a fuller's soap to cleanse the wool.

These are all very practical, everyday tasks. Preparing for the coming of the Christ may not take unusual or complicated or hard-to-think of ways. The task of preparing is right before us in our everyday lives.

Look for it daily, do it daily as we prepare. The light from the second Advent candle can help us put into action our preparation.

Lighting of the Second Advent Candle

Unison Prayer

Come to us, O Holy God, as we prepare for your coming. It is difficult sometimes for us to prepare for this miraculous event in our frantic and complicated lives. Help us to seek ways in our everyday, ordinary lives to show that we follow the light. Amen.

Children's Sermon Starter

Ask the children to share ways that they are told to "get ready," such as to get ready for school, or dinner, or church, or bed. Ask how they do that. Do they change clothes, wash up, gather their books, and so forth. Talk with them about the fuller washing the wool after it is shorn from the sheep. The fuller is preparing the wool, getting it ready.

Link this to getting ready for Advent—the coming of Jesus. See if together you can think of ideas that they can do to prepare for this event.

Close with prayer that the children can find ways in their daily lives during Advent to get ready for Jesus' coming.

Offering Prayer

One of the ways we show our readiness for your coming, O God, is to offer to you these gifts. Use them to prepare the world for your reign so that all your people will know the good news of your love. Bless these gifts and bless us as we offer them to you. Amen.

Communion Prayer

Prepare our hearts for the coming of our Savior, dear God. Straighten out the rough places in our attitudes, fill with your love the low places of fear and depression, tear down the hills of prejudice and pride. Here at this table may our spirits commune with your Spirit, so that your Spirit may touch and influence our lives. Bless this bread, so that in the eating of it, we may participate in Christ's body, given for us.

Bless this cup, so that in drinking it we are led in the paths of peace. Amen.

BENEDICTION AND BLESSING *(Philippians 1:9–11)*

As you go in light, may your love overflow more and more with knowledge and insight to help you determine what is best, so in the day of Christ you may be pure and blameless, having produced the harvest of righteousness that comes though Jesus Christ for the glory and praise of God.

Third Sunday of Advent

Zephaniah 3:14-20. Isaiah 12:2-6. Philippians 4:4-7. Luke 3:7-18.

LITANY OF LIGHT *(from Philippians 4)*

> LEADER: We walk as a people of light. We are preparing for the coming of Christ. Let us hear words that will give us help as we wait.
>
> MEN: Rejoice in the Lord!
>
> CHILDREN: Be gentle to everyone.
>
> **ALL: Know that the Lord is near.**
>
> WOMEN: Do not worry; let God know our needs.
>
> **ALL: Be thankful. The Lord is near. The Lord is coming!**

LIGHTING OF PREVIOUS SUNDAYS' CANDLES

MEDITATION

Do you ever remember saying to your parents, "I'm bored! What can I do?" Perhaps the answer wasn't what you expected. Most of us were hoping for something exciting to do, a new toy or game, or for our parents even to say, "I have just the thing—let's go to the movies…or the zoo…"

But most of the time that just didn't happen. More than likely, it was something like this, "Well, if you're really bored, do your homework." Or, "Maybe this is the time to clean your room…or the garage." Aargh! That wasn't what we wanted to hear at all. We wanted fun, not *responsibility.*

When the Messiah comes, there will be a change. The Christ will teach us how to live in a different way. We as Christians will begin to act responsibly. We will need to share, be honest. What better way to prepare for the Coming than to practice responsibility right now—in our lives today, and the rest of our lives.

The growing light of the Advent wreath with three candles lit can help us walk responsibly in the light.

LIGHTING OF THE THIRD ADVENT CANDLE

UNISON PRAYER

As we wait for your coming, God of salvation, help us to know what to do, and to act upon it. Help us to be firm in our commitment to you so that others will come to you and your Son, our Savior. Amen.

CHILDREN'S SERMON STARTER

Read to the children verse 10 from Luke 3: "And the crowds asked him, 'What then should we do?'" Tell them a bit of the background about John the Baptist and his mission. Share with the children that John answered, telling the people to be honest and fair with each other and to share with others. Let them know that these are ways that they can act in their lives too. Remind them that during this third week of Advent, they can help prepare for Christ's coming by their actions. Close with prayer that the children will be guided in their actions and will feel God with them.

OFFERING PRAYER

God, who challenges our lives to be filled with honesty, fairness, and sharing, we bring our gifts to you with joy, in response to your asking. Bless them as we are blessed in the giving. Amen.

COMMUNION PRAYER

God of justice and love, how easy it is to stray from the paths you have set before us. We are tempted by prejudice, fear, self-righteousness, and greed. Yet when we stray, you call us back through your word. We come to this table seeking to be true to your way. With repentant hearts, we eat the bread and drink the cup that you have given us. Help us learn to be more faithful and more loving. Open our hearts, so that we may receive the Christ you send us. Guide us by your Spirit that we may stay on your paths. Amen.

BENEDICTION AND BLESSING *(Philippians 4:7)*

Go, walk in the light. Act as people of God. The Lord is near. And the peace of God, which surpasses all understanding, will guard your hearts and your minds in Jesus Christ. Amen.

Fourth Sunday of Advent

Micah 5:2–5a. Luke 1:47–55 or Psalm 80:1–7.
Hebrews 10:5–10. Luke 1:39–45.

LITANY OF LIGHT

The birth of our Lord is near. Our waiting is almost over.
**We have tried to live this Advent season as children
of God. We have tried to take God's words seriously
and to change our lives in preparation for the coming
of God's Son.**
In the name of God the Creator and in the name of Jesus
who comes, let us celebrate our preparation! Let us, like
Mary, rejoice in God our Savior.

LIGHTING OF PREVIOUS SUNDAYS' CANDLES

MEDITATION

We have all learned about opposites. Help me out here.
Hot (cold), dry (wet), dark (light), little (big). That's right.
And with opposites come contrasts.

Micah's scripture for today reads, "But you, O Bethlehem
of Ephrathah, who are one of the *little* clans of Judah." What
an insult! But Micah doesn't let this story end on such a
negative note. He doesn't give Bethlehem time to be discouraged. In the next breath he tells them that they will be
responsible for one who is to come who will rule Israel. An
ordinary, sleepy little town, a little clan, of no significance.
And in Luke's scripture we hear Mary praise God, for "he
has looked with favor on the *lowliness* of his servant."

God didn't choose the more significant city of Jerusalem
or the daughter of a rich and famous person to bring forth
the Messiah. God chose the opposite of what was expected.
God chose an ordinary town and an ordinary woman.

During this Advent season, we have learned how to live
as one who knows God, who knows the Christ. As we reflect
back, it isn't the big events, the earthshaking decisions, the
world-famous people that make the difference in a Christlike

60

life. It is exactly the opposite. It is in the everyday, maybe mundane, repetitious, ordinary things in our lives where, as children of light, we can make a difference. We are God's people.

LIGHTING OF THE FOURTH ADVENT CANDLE

UNISON PRAYER

Thank you, God of ordinary times and people, for helping us learn that our role in your kingdom is in how we live our lives day by day in the light of your love. Amen.

CHILDREN'S SERMON STARTER

Ask the children if they have ever wanted to be someone famous—the President, a TV or movie star, a well-known musician, a cartoon character. Have them share how being famous might make a difference. Help them remember that Mary the mother of Jesus was not a famous person, but an ordinary young woman whom God chose. Tell them that each of us ordinary people (children) has been chosen by God to do God's work. Pray with them that as Christmas is near, each of us will find ways to do God's work.

OFFERING PRAYER

With these ordinary gifts of our lives, our talents, and our financial contributions, you work miracles, O Lord of life. Use these gifts we bring to you so that all may know your saving grace. Amen.

COMMUNION PRAYER

Shepherd us, dear God. Guide us and protect us. Prepare our hearts to be open to the love that you have to give. Bring to our hearts the joy of knowing your promise, the promise fulfilled in Jesus Christ, our Savior. We come to your table to eat the bread and drink the cup that remind us why Christ came to earth. Bless us with your Spirit's presence as we receive the precious gift of love. Amen.

BENEDICTION AND BLESSING   *(from Hebrews 10)*

It is by God's will that we have been made holy through the offering of the body of Jesus Christ once for all. Go, in peace, and lead holy lives as Christ has taught. Go into the world carrying the light.

Christmas Eve

(Any of the following scriptures may be used
on Christmas Eve or Christmas Day.)

Isaiah 9:2–7	*Isaiah 62:6–12*	*Isaiah 52:7–10*
Psalm 96	*Psalm 97*	*Psalm 98*
Titus 2:11–14	*Titus 3:4–7*	*Hebrews 1:1–4, 5–12*
Luke 2:1–14, 15–20	*Luke 2:1–7, 8–20*	*John 1:1–14*

LITANY OF LIGHT *(from John 1)*

In the beginning was the Word, and the Word was with
God, and the Word was God.
**He was in the beginning with God. All things came
into being through him, and without him not one
thing came into being.**
What has come into being in him was life, and the life was
the light of all people.
**The light shines in the darkness, and the darkness
did not overcome it.**

LIGHTING OF PREVIOUS SUNDAYS' CANDLES

MEDITATION

We see them every day. They help us get around town.
They help us find new places. They direct us to places to
eat. We follow them all the time. What are they? They are
directional signs: "4th Street exit 2 ½ miles"; "Historical Site
2 miles south"; "Murphy's Burger Barn 3 blocks ahead";
"First Church—north 2 blocks." Without them to help us
find our way, getting around would be much more difficult.

In John's gospel, that is exactly what John the Baptist
was. He was a directional sign pointing to Jesus, the Word.
The author of the gospel tells us that the Word had been
there from the beginning. But God in his wisdom sent John
the Baptist to witness to the Word—to point to the Word.
Without his directional sign, we could have missed the Word.

John the Baptist pointed to the Word, Jesus Christ, God's
Son, by signs saying, "Repent"; "The one who comes after
me is more powerful than I am"; "The kingdom of heaven

63

has come near"; "I will baptize you with water, but the one who is coming will baptize you with the spirit." John the Baptist challenged lifestyles by telling people, "You must share your food and clothing; you must not collect more than is due to you. Do not threaten or accuse wrongly."

These signs, directional signs, point to Christ, the Word. Just as we follow signs to exits on highways or to a fast food restaurant or to a historical sight or church, we follow signs from the witness to the Word, John the Baptist, toward the Word, Jesus Christ our Savior.

Follow the signs, meet the Christ, and walk in the light.

LIGHTING OF THE CHRIST CANDLE

UNISON PRAYER

**"We rejoice in the light, and we echo the song
that comes down through the night
from the heavenly throng,
and we welcome the glorious gospel they bring,
and we greet in the cradle our savior and king."[1]
Thank you God of light for your Word, Jesus our
Savior. Amen.**

CHILDREN'S SERMON STARTER

(See the selections for Christmas Eve from the section at the end of this book entitled "Lighting the Advent Candles during the Children's Sermon Time.")

COMMUNION PRAYER

You spoke the word, Creator God, and the universe came into being. You spoke the word, and life filled our planet. You spoke the word, and people received the covenant and the law to guide them. Tonight *(Today)* we remember that you spoke the word, and the word became flesh and dwelt among us. We thank you for the Christ, who came into our presence, as a baby, grew up, walked among us, healed, taught, and offered his life for us. The bread we eat reminds us that Christ is our living bread. The cup we drink helps us recall the love that was poured out for us in Christ's birth, life, and death. Yet this is more than a memorial; it is a celebration that the Christ who came into our midst became the risen Christ and is here with us. We rejoice in your word that made us, that came to us, and that is with us now. Fill us with your Spirit on this Christmas Eve (*Day*). Amen.

OFFERING PRAYER

On this evening (*day*) we recognize that all life is a gift from you, good and generous God. All good things come from your graciousness. Especially, we remember your gift of Jesus Christ, who came to show us your way. Bless these offerings we give now, so that through them others might come to know your love. Help our spirits grow in generosity and graciousness as we attempt to grow into the Spirit of the one whose birth we celebrate. Amen.

BENEDICTION AND BLESSING

> "Be thou a bright flame before me,
> Be thou a guiding star above me,
> Be thou a smooth path below me,
> Be thou a kindly shepherd behind me,
> Today—tonight—and forever."[2]

---

[1]"There's a Song in the Air!" by Josiah G. Holland (1879).
[2]Columba of Iona, circa 521–597.

— Sunday after Christmas Day

1 Samuel 2:18–20, 26. Psalm 148.
Colossians 3:12–17. Luke 2:41–52.

LITANY OF LIGHT *(from Psalm 148)*

As children of God who have seen again the coming of
Jesus the Christ, how do we respond?
**We respond with praise: Praise the LORD! Praise the
LORD from the heavens;
Praise him in the heights!
Praise him, all his angels; praise him, all his host!**
Kings of the earth and all peoples, princes and all rulers
of earth! Young men and women alike, old and young
together!
**Let us praise the name of the LORD, for his name
alone is exalted; his glory is above earth and heaven.
Praise the LORD!**

LIGHTING OF ALL THE CANDLES

MEDITATION

The week after Christmas is a strange time, isn't it? It
seems hard to say exactly how we are feeling. The excitement and preparation are over. The exhaustion may have
hit hard. Leftover food just isn't as exciting to smell and
taste as it was the first time around. The tree at home has
lost its enchantment as the packages underneath it have
been opened.

Sometimes there is a letdown, disappointment. We have
been so busy preparing for the details of a family Christmas
celebration that when it is over, well, it is over. We have
been so busy with the Advent preparations at church and
with enjoying the loveliness of the Christmas decorations
that to think of a sanctuary without all the special light and
color seems depressing. It will be, as the expression goes,
"same old, same old."

But it is in the ordinary time of the year that the message of Advent and Christmas really lives! Try to remember some of the scriptures that were read during Advent that helped us prepare for the Coming in our everyday lives. Those instructions are not just for Advent, but for all year.

As we come to the close of Christmas, let's not come to the close of the Christmas celebration. Let's each of us remember the instructions we were given to prepare for the Messiah. Let's remember to do them. And during the year, like the young boy Samuel and the young boy Jesus, we too can grow and find favor with God and God's people.

UNISON PRAYER

With grateful hearts, God and Father of the Christ, we praise you for your wonderful gift to us of your Son, our Savior. Help us to live every day of our lives witnessing that we know you. Amen.

CHILDREN'S SERMON STARTER

Ask the children what they remember most about the Advent and Christmas celebrations at church this year. Was it the candles being lit each week, the familiar music, the Christmas program, or something else? Will these things be harder to remember as the decorations in the sanctuary are put away or as the weather warms? See if together you can share ways that they can remember this special time of year, all year. Close with a prayer of thanksgiving that God's Son, Jesus, is with us all year.

OFFERING PRAYER

As we go from preparing for the coming of the Christ to the celebration of your Son's birth, we go in praise for the great things you have done, O giving God. We offer our praise to you in these gifts. We pray that all your people will know your great love for them as these gifts are used for your reign. Amen.

Everlasting Light

COMMUNION PRAYER

Teach us your ways, O God of wisdom. Help us remember that no matter how young or old we are, we can still grow in faith, love, and grace. Let this table be a place where we can learn the ways of Christ. Let the bread we eat and the wine we drink help us learn that the boy in the temple became the man in the upper room. Through your Spirit, help us celebrate the presence of the living Christ with us. Amen.

CARRYING FORTH THE LIGHT

(This Sunday the acolyte should relight the taper just before extinguishing the Christ candle, which is the last to be extinguished. As the acolyte goes back down the center aisle, those who are able should rise as the light passes.)

BENEDICTION AND BLESSING *(from Colossians 3:12–17)*

As God's chosen ones, clothe yourselves with compassion, kindness, humility, meekness, and patience. Forgive each other. Clothe yourselves with love. Let the peace of Christ rule in your hearts. Be thankful. Let the word of Christ dwell in you richly. Whatever you do, in word or deed, do everything in the name of the Lord Jesus, giving thanks to God the Father through him. Amen.

Christmas Sunday

(For Year A, B, or C, when Christmas Day is on Sunday)
*(Any of the following scriptures may be used
on Christmas Eve or Christmas Day.)*

Isaiah 9:2–7	*Isaiah 62:6–12*	*Isaiah 52:7–10*
Psalm 96	*Psalm 97*	*Psalm 98*
Titus 2:11–14	*Titus 3:4–7*	*Hebrews 1:1–4, 5–12*
Luke 2:1–14, 15–20	*Luke 2:1–7, 8–20*	*John 1:1–14*

LITANY OF LIGHT *(from Psalm 98)*

O, sing to the LORD a new song, for he has done marvelous things.

He has remembered his steadfast love and faithfulness to the house of Israel.

Make a joyful noise to the LORD, all the earth; break forth into joyous song and sing praises.

WOMEN: Sing praises to the LORD with the lyre, with the lyre and the sound of melody.

MEN: With trumpets and the sound of the horn make a joyful noise before the King, the LORD.

Sing to the LORD a new song, for he has done marvelous things! Christ our Savior has come!

LIGHTING OF PREVIOUS SUNDAYS' CANDLES

MEDITATION

It is a very special day when Christmas Day is also a Sunday! What a wonderful celebration to come together in God's house for Sunday worship on the day of God's Son's birth.

There is a story of two women in the delivery room. One was in labor with her second child. Her close friend had gone with her to be present at the birth to coach her and support her at this very special time. The mother pushed, and in a holy, miraculous moment her child was born.

The friend, awed by the process, went to tell the waiting family about the new baby. "What is it?" they asked eagerly.

"A baby! A baby!" was all the excited friend could say.

Today is born—what else?—a baby…a baby who has changed, and is changing, and will change the world and each individual person in it. Even though we have heard the Christmas story countless times, it is new again each time. Each time we experience the Christmas story, our lives are made new by the baby who is the Christ. We are given renewed hope in knowing God's love for us.

We can experience God's word made flesh, dwelling among us, Emmanuel. We can experience God's Word made flesh, full of grace and truth. We can experience God's Word made flesh for us, our Savior! And what do we say when asked about Christmas? We too say, "A baby! A baby!"

LIGHTING OF THE CHRIST CANDLE

UNISON PRAYER

Today, God, we celebrate the greatest gift we could ever be given, a gift that has the power to transform our lives. We thank you for your Son, our Savior. Help us use your gift to transform the lives of others, that they will know you and your love. Amen.

CHILDREN'S SERMON STARTER

Ask if the children can remember their families' telling them about the time they were born. Do they remember hearing the stories from parents or grandparents? See if any child can tell the story of his or her birth. Share with them the excitement that comes with a birth, the awe that comes when seeing a child for the very first time, the miracle that God makes. Then ask what birth we are celebrating today. Jesus', of course. Tell them that we are also excited about this birth because it shows God's great love for each of us. Nothing can be greater than a parent's love for a child; nothing is greater than God's love for God's children. Close with prayer that the children will celebrate with excitement the birth of Jesus and feel God's love.

OFFERING PRAYER

In the darkness of that holy night, a child who is our Savior is born. And from the darkness of that holy night, we receive the gift that will overcome that darkness. O God of light, we thank you for illuminating our lives. Because we are children of the light, we now offer our gifts to you. We pray that these gifts will bring light to all parts of your world and to all your people. Amen.

COMMUNION PRAYER

"Blessed art thou, O Christmas Christ,
that thy cradle was so low that shepherds,
poorest and simplest of earthly folk,
could yet kneel beside it,
and look level-eyed into the face of God."[1]
We see you, God, in the Christ you send to us today;
we know that the gift of your Son
is for all your people.
At this table, we gather
in greatest thanksgiving for this gift.
The bread and wine that we will take now
to celebrate the Christ's birth,
we will also take to commemorate his death
and to celebrate his resurrection.
Like those shepherds of many years ago,
we are in awe in your presence
as we also see you. Amen.

BENEDICTION AND BLESSING *(from Titus 2)*

The grace of God has appeared, bringing salvation to all. We have waited. Christ has come. Amen.

---

[1]Janet Morley, ed., *Bread of Tomorrow* (Maryknoll, New York: Orbis Press, 1992), p. 45.

ADDITIONAL RESOURCES

Lighting the Advent Candles during the Children's Sermon Time

There may be times in which a congregation will choose to light the Advent candles during the children's sermon. *Everlasting Light* contains three sets of services provided for these occasions. These were previously published in *Partners in Prayer* over several years.[1]

These children's sermons do not follow the lectionary, but rather follow familiar parts of the scriptures that the children may hear read during Advent. The tone of these messages is a conversational style, indicating participation by the children. If you choose to use these, eliminate the meditation and the children's sermon starter from *Everlasting Light,* but use all other elements of the service.

Set 1

Set 1 uses the lovely carol by Mary Anne Parrott, "One Candle Is Lit," *Chalice Hymnal* no. 128. It is set to the tune "Cradle Song." If your congregation does not have a hymnal with this tune, it may be sung also to "Away in a Manger." Permission to reprint the words in the bulletin so the congregation may join in the singing is given by Chalice Press. Please note this permission in the bulletin: "'One Candle Is Lit,' words by Mary Anne Parrott, 1988. Copyright 1995 by Chalice Press. Used by permission."

First Sunday of Advent

Thanksgiving is just over and already we are thinking about Christmas. The stores have been decorated for weeks. Have you heard Christmas songs as you have shopped or listened to the radio? In worship this morning, we will light an Advent candle for the first time. Maybe your home is also beginning to look like Christmas is coming.

Have you heard the fun Christmas song, "Here Comes Santa Claus"? Who else comes at Christmas? You're right! Jesus Christ comes at Christmas.

When someone is coming, we wait for their arrival. Sometimes waiting is hard because we are impatient. Jesus is worth waiting for! God's people waited and hoped for many, many years for the birth of the Christ.

Read Psalm 130:5–8. When Jesus comes, we see that all our hoping and waiting have been worthwhile.

Sing together:

> "Come surely, Lord Jesus, as dawn follows night,
> our hearts long to greet you, as roses, the light.
> Salvation, draw near us, our vision engage.
> One candle is lit for the hope of the age."

Light the first Advent candle.

Pray: O God, who comes to us in Jesus Christ, help us wait for your coming through all the days. Let us feel the hope that your presence brings. Amen.

Second Sunday of Advent

Light the first Advent candle.

What has your family done this week to get ready for Christmas? Another way to say "get ready" is *prepare.* Maybe your family is preparing for Christmas by sending cards or planning a family celebration. Are you preparing for a Christmas program at church by learning new songs? Last week we talked about Jesus' coming. *Advent* means *coming.*

Some special ways to prepare for Jesus' coming are to think about and work for God's love and peace. How can you work for peace in God's name? Collecting food for a food bank or clothes for the homeless is one way. Treating all God's people with kindness is a way. Not watching TV shows that have shooting or other violence in them is another way to prepare for God's peace.

Read Micah 4:1–2a, 6:8. As we learn ways of peace, we are preparing for Jesus' coming.

Sing together:

> "Come quickly, shalom, teach us how to prepare
> for a gift that compels us with justice to care.
> Our spirits are restless till sin and war cease.
> One candle is lit for the reign of God's peace."

Light the second Advent candle.

Pray: Jesus, you come to teach us peace; help us to learn your ways and to walk in your paths of peace and justice. Amen.

Third Sunday of Advent

Light the first two Advent candles.

Have you ever seen a fireworks show at the end of a hot summer holiday? They reach high, and we ooh and aah over their bright colors against the dark night sky. It is a real celebration!

The birth of Jesus is a real celebration too. It is a joyous time. God's people had waited and prepared for the birth of the Messiah for many years. Then came the day when Jesus was born. Can you remember what the angels told the shepherds?

Read Luke 2:8–15. They gathered to sing their joy at this event! What are ways you can celebrate during Advent? Singing, praying, and being excited over the coming of Jesus are good ways to celebrate.

Sing together:

> "Come, festively sing while awaiting the birth,
> join angels in dancing from heaven to earth.
> Wave banners of good news, lift high thankful praise.
> One candle is lit for the joy of these days."

Light the third Advent candle.

Pray: We are filled with joy, O God of love, as we await the celebration of the birth of your son. Help us share our joy with all people by the things we do and say. Amen.

Fourth Sunday of Advent

Light the first three Advent candles.

How many of you have had a surprise that was really fun? Maybe you planned a surprise party for someone else. Or maybe you were the one surprised!

God planned a surprise. For hundreds of years, God's people were expecting a Savior. They thought it would be a king or a powerful ruler. Do you know what happened? That's right. God's surprise to the people was a Savior who came first as a baby. Our God plans many wonderful surprises for us, things we don't expect to happen.

Read Isaiah 11:6–10. Those verses are full of surprises: wild and tame animals living together, a child leading the animals, a child not being hurt by a harmful snake. We don't expect these things to happen.

But with God, surprises are possible! We have waited and prepared. We have celebrated, and now we can see the wonderful surprise God has for us in Jesus Christ!

Sing together:

"Come, wander where lion and lamb gently play,
where evil is banished and faith takes the day,
a babe in a manger to fool the world's eyes.
One candle is lit for God's loving surprise."

Light the fourth Advent candle.

Pray: We wait so excitedly for your coming now, Jesus. Help us to see God's surprises in our lives. We love you, Jesus. Be with all our families and friends through this week. Amen.

Christmas Eve

Light the four Advent candles.

It is finally here! This is Christmas Eve. All the hoping, preparing, and celebrating have been worth it. Jesus will come just as we hoped. God does not disappoint God's people.

How are you celebrating? We are here at a special church service tonight. Are all the Advent candles lit on the big wreath in the front of the sanctuary?

Today our reading from the Bible is the Christmas story.

Read Luke 2:1–21. Listen to the wonderful words telling us of Jesus' birth. From the surprise of our Savior coming as a baby, God has plans for us. When we learn from Jesus' teachings, we begin to know the love that God has for each of us. Several months from now, we will celebrate again. At that time we will celebrate the resurrection of Jesus Christ. We know God loves us!

Everlasting Light

Sing together:

"Come, listen, the sounds of God with us ring clear,
and signs of a cross in the distance appear.
The Word once made flesh, yet the Word ever near,
One candle is lit for the Christ birthday here."

Light the Christ candle.

Until next Advent, show God's love in your lives by your actions.

Pray: God, we know you are with us, so we call you Emmanuel. Thank you for your presence all the days of our lives. Thank you for sending us Jesus Christ so that we will know your love. Amen.

Set 2

First Sunday of Advent

Have you every wanted to be bigger or older or more important than you think you are? If you are four, are you excited about being five so you can go to school? If you are eight, are you anxious to be twelve so you can go to the movies with friends instead of your parents? If you are twelve, can you hardly wait to be sixteen so you can drive? Is there a special toy or bike that you think would make you feel more important? Ask your parents or grandparents the same questions. Maybe they would like to have a promotion at work; or maybe they would like a new car or a big new house to make them feel important.

Read Luke 1:46–55. God found Mary. She wasn't anyone important, just a young girl from an ordinary family. But God chose her to be the mother of Jesus, the Christ! Even though we are perhaps younger than we want to be, or less important than we would like to be, God has a purpose for each of us.

Light the first Advent candle.

Pray together: Thank you, God, for making each of us special in your eyes. Help us each see your purpose for us. We thank you for Mary, the mother of Jesus. As Christmas comes, let us remember we are celebrating the birth of the Christ child. Amen.

Second Sunday of Advent

Light the first Advent candle.

Have you ever been to a zoo or a wildlife refuge and seen the wolves? They look fierce with their long faces, pointed short ears, and bright eyes. Back in Bible times wolves were an enemy of the sheep. The wolves would gather in packs and attack the sheep and lambs.

Read Isaiah 11:1–6. This is hard to believe, isn't it? (*Reread verse 6.*) The person who wrote this is saying that the wolf, the enemy of the sheep, will live with them. That isn't all. Other animals that you wouldn't think of living together *will* live together. And who shall lead them? Yes, a child.

These verses from the Bible are full of surprises, aren't they? God's story is full of surprises, and the best one of all is Jesus' being born at Christmastime!

Light the second Advent candle.

Pray together: For all the surprises at Christmas, we give you thanks. Help us remember that we are big enough and important enough to see all the surprises that you give us, God. Amen.

Third Sunday of Advent

Light the first two Advent candles.

This is the third week we have come together to light the Advent candles. Are you excited? Is your house being decorated with a tree and other Christmas items? Have you been buying presents? Are there surprises under the tree yet? Is it hard to wait?

Read Luke 2:1–6. This is the Christmas story. You have heard it many times. Do you hear about any waiting in this story? Mary and Joseph waited nine months for Jesus to be born. They waited until they could get to Bethlehem to pay the taxes. Although it is not mentioned in this part of the story, the Jewish people had waited many, many years for the Savior to be born. You are not the only ones to wait for Christmas!

The Jews who waited for the Christ to come and Mary and Joseph did not just sit and wait, and many Christians today don't either. They are busy doing God's work. I imagine you, too, can find work to do during the rest of Advent—work that is God's work.

Light the third Advent candle.

Pray together: God, help us wait for your Son's coming by doing work for you. Let us see what you want us to do. Amen.

Fourth Sunday of Advent

Light the first three Advent candles.

Do you remember the first time you saw something under a magnifying glass? Did you say, "That couldn't-be that tiny bug. It's too big!" But then, you looked at the tiny bug again under the magnifying glass and realized that it was the same bug. The lens in the glass made such a tiny thing big! A cactus spine under a microscope reveals sharp barbs on the needles. It is hard to believe something that tiny and fuzzy could be so pointed and barbed!

Read Luke 1:46–48. Mary is saying that her soul magnifies the Lord. Her small, humble spirit, that of a young, poor girl, magnifies the Lord because she has been chosen to be the mother of a very special child.

In God's eyes, small things become important. Remember the magnifying glass? The smallest things we do for God are magnified. As your family serves God in your daily lives, it is magnified by God to be **very important!**

Light the fourth Advent candle.

Pray together: Help us always to find ways to serve you, God. We know that our efforts are always important to you. We thank you for helping us see that we are worthy in your sight. Amen.

Christmas Eve

Light all four Advent candles.

Christmas Eve is finally here! We have waited and prepared during the four weeks of Advent for this night to come. Tonight or tomorrow many of you will have family celebrations of presents and a special meal. Perhaps you will join with family you don't see very often.

Read Luke 2:8–14. On the night Christ was born the shepherds had a celebration too. The angels came to them and said, "Do not be afraid. I am bringing you and everyone else good news. In the city of Bethlehem, a Savior is born. He is the Messiah." Then the angels celebrated and sang to the shepherds,

"Glory to God in the highest and on earth peace among all peoples."

Light the Christ candle.

We may never have angels sing to us. But we can celebrate the birthday of Jesus the Messiah. And we can work for peace. We can celebrate that peace each time our families solve a problem fairly. We can celebrate that peace that Christ gives each time justice is given to those who are treated unfairly. We can celebrate that peace when countries work problems out rather than having a war. See how many celebrations of peace you can have before next Christmas!

Pray together: We thank you, God, for this special Christmas. Help us always to remember we are important and big in your plan for us. Let us celebrate your peace often. Amen.

Set 3

First Sunday of Advent

Do you remember playing outdoors on a hot summer day in the sandbox, on the swing set, with your trucks or bike? Then at the end of the day, your mom or dad called you in and said, "It's bath time!" What happened when the soap washed you clean? I imagine you could see how much cleaner your hands, arms, legs, and feet became as you washed.

Read Malachi 3:1–4. This is hard to understand, isn't it? Did you hear the words, "fuller's soap"? After a sheep has been sheared, a *fuller* is the person who cleans the wool to prepare it for spinning. You were becoming cleaner as you got ready for bed. Both you and the fuller were preparing for something. The Old Testament messenger was telling us how to get ready for the coming of the Lord. During Advent we prepare for Jesus' birth.

Light the first Advent candle.

With the brightness of the candle flame, think with your family about ways to prepare for Jesus' coming to each of us.

Pray: O great and giving God, thank you for giving us time to prepare for your coming so we may celebrate the real reason for Christmas. Amen.

Second Sunday of Advent

Light the first Advent candle.

Can you think of a time when you really knew that your mom and dad or grandfather or grandmother loved you? Maybe it was something special they said to you or because of a gift they gave you or a wonderful time you had together.

Read Hosea 11:1–9. In this Old Testament reading we hear how much God loved Israel. Israel was a country—God's chosen people—whom God loved as a parent loves a child. Listen for these ways God loved Israel: God called the child, taught the child to walk, took the child in God's arms, healed the child, and fed the child.

We know our parents love us by the way they care for us; we know God's love for us because of the way God cares for us. Especially during Advent, as we prepare for Jesus' coming, and at Christmas we know God's love because God loves us enough to give us Jesus, God's son.

Light the second Advent candle.

With the brightness of the candle flame, remember how you are preparing during Advent for Christ's coming and think of the many ways you know God's love.

Pray: Thank you, God, for the ways our parents love us and especially the ways you love and care for us. Thank you for Jesus, who shows us your love. Amen.

Third Sunday of Advent

Light the first two Advent candles.

Once a family planned to go on a summer vacation. The mom and dad packed clothes for themselves and the children and pillows, toys, and snacks for the children. They planned to take their pet dog, so they also packed dog food, a leash, and water for the dog.

Early in the morning they loaded the car with all the suitcases and other things they needed for the trip. The children got in the car, the mom and dad got in, everyone buckled their seat belts, and off they went. As they backed out of the driveway, they could see the forlorn face of their dog looking out the living room window; they had forgotten her! Of course, they pulled back in the driveway and opened the front door. Out the dog bounded! She wasn't about to be forgotten. The family wouldn't have gone very far before they would have remembered their pet. But they were sad to have forgotten her at all.

Read Luke 1:67–72. This gospel reading tells of many things that God has done throughout the many years to help God's people. (*Read the last part of verse 72 again*) "...and has remembered his holy covenant." God will always remember us as God has always remembered God's people. Covenant means promise. God does what God has promised to do!

Light the third Advent candle.

With the brightness of the candle flame, think with your family about ways that you know God remembers you. At Christmas we know God will not forget us as we see preparations for Christmas and remember God's love in Jesus.

Pray: Thank you, God, for always remembering us. We know we are loved. Amen.

Fourth Sunday of Advent

Light the first three Advent candles.

Three of our Advent candles are already lit, and today we will light the fourth. Christmas is coming very soon. Let's remember why we have lit the other candles: to prepare for Jesus, to show us how much Jesus loves us, and to remind us that God remembers us always.

Did your parents ever give you a chance to earn some money by doing chores, like taking out trash, putting away dishes or laundry, or helping to clean the house? Then, when you were done with the chores, you were paid.

Read 1 John 4:7–12. This letter tells more about God's love. What is important is in verse 11. God loves us before we ever love God. Because God loves us, God sent Jesus. God didn't send Jesus because we earned him, the way we earn money by doing chores. God sent Jesus simply because God loves us. There is nothing we can do to earn this Christmas gift of Jesus.

Light the fourth Advent candle.

With the brightness of the candle flame, think about how we can show our thanksgiving for this wonderful love.

Pray: Thank you, God, for giving us your love in Jesus. Amen.

Christmas Eve

Light the first four Advent candles.

Read Luke 2:15–21. Tonight we celebrate the most special of all holidays. Christmas Eve! What are we celebrating? Right! the birth of Jesus Christ. God shows God's love for all people by giving us the most wonderful Christmas present—God's own son.

Reread verse 20. The shepherds went back praising God for what they had seen. We can do the same all year! Tonight we celebrate Jesus' birth again as we do every Christmas. And we can celebrate all year long in a wonderful way that shows God's love by glorifying and praising God in everything we do.

Light the Christ candle.

The brightly lit Advent wreath with all the candles glowing can remind us to celebrate God's love.

Pray: God of Jesus, our Savior, help us to remember this light during the year until Advent comes again. Thank you for your great love. Amen.

[1]St. Louis: Chalice Press, 1992, 1994, 1996.